COVID-19
THE ROLE OF THE STATE

Connor Court Quarterly *Number 13 - 2020*

Published by Connor Court Publishing Pty Ltd, 2020.

Copyright © As a collection, Connor Court Publishing.

CONNOR COURT PUBLISHING PTY LTD
PO Box 7257
Redland Bay QLD 4165
sales@connorcourt.com
www.connorcourtpublishing.com.au

ISBN: 9781925826982 (pbk.)

All images within the Quarterly are taken from Wikipedia Commons.

Cover design by Ian James.

Printed in Australia.

PREVIOUS ISSUE OF THE CONNOR COURT QUARTERLY

Connor Court Quarterly, Volume 12

- Was Australia Discovered by De Quiros in the Year 1606? -- Cardinal Patrick Moran
- Book Launch: 'The Heart of James McAuley' by Peter Coleman -- Tony Staley, Tony Abbott, Peter Coleman
- Vale Roger Sworder -- Brian Coman

www.connorcourtpublishing.com.au

EDITORIAL

GOVERNMENTS ARE BAD FOR BUSINESS

"Death is all around us, but we live life as if it is eternal". This, I am guessing, was the motto that governments across the world took on when pushing forward with lockdowns as a result of the COVID-19 pandemic.

This issue of the Connor Court Quarterly is dedicated to the COVID-19 pandemic, the lockdowns and the role of the State in responding to the crisis.

COVID-19 has virtually closed down society. In Victoria, as one example, people are essentially under house arrest. Yet, with the rate of deaths so low (in Australia) I'm perplexed at the lack of scrutiny on the lockdowns.

Now, we are in no way denying that the virus has the potential to kill, particularly the elderly and those with a compromised immune systems, but does the ends, in this instance, justify the means?

In early March, I was in Melbourne, doing book launches and conducting various meetings with authors. In one of those meeting, I caught up with the one of our authors. This author, in his eighties, was clearly concerned about his health, but still agreed to meet, although briefly. We agreed at the meeting to delay his publication until concerns over the virus had passed over. He told me that he was going into a voluntarily isolation. I respected his decision and thought he had made a wise, voluntary decision on the future of his health.

His decision was made without the help of Jenny Mitakos, the Victorian Health Minister or Dan Andrews, the Victorian State Premier.

I then proceeded to go to the State Library, where I usually go and sit down in the foyer inbetween meetings and use their free Wi-Fi while I prepare for my next meeting. Normally, I struggle to find a seat, but on this day, apart from one other person, the place was virtually empty. People, had voluntarily decided to stay away. People were concerned about their health. Once again, this was done without any State sanctioned laws. People exercising caution without government issued directives.

Therefore, I was aghast, when I arrived back to Brisbane, to hear that State borders were closed and in some states, like Victoria and NSW, there was a full lockdown. Let us not mentioned New Zealand, which has left us all for dead when it comes to an over-reaction!

Now months later, like little children, we are being told what we can and cannot do, despite the death toll in Australia being ridiculously low. In the few cases of death that have occurred in Australia it has generally been the elderly. Despite the over-zealous Victorian health minister, reminding people that this is not only an old person's disease. The fact is, and it clearly has shown in Australia, young people may contract the disease, but in most cases it will be asymptomatic.

This *Connor Court Quarterly*, looks at the role of the State in enforcing remedies to tackle the virus especially in subjecting its citizens to a full scale lockdown. Jeffrey Tucker, Editorial Director of the American Institute for Economic Research, and the author of the *Friedman Papers*, has been a staunch critic on the measures adopted by governments across the world. Mark Hendrickx, author of *A Guide to Climbing Ayers Rocks*, compares the COVID-19 virus and its aftermath with the SARS outbreak back in 2009 where Kevin Rudd and Nicola Roxan tackled the problem without imposing draconian laws and directives.

Finally, Daniel Wild tackles the elephant in the room. If we are all in this together tackling COVID-19, why hasn't the public sector taken a hit, with sacrifices like those in the private sector. He also lays out a practical plan for regrowth after this government-inflicted disaster that shares the burden between the private and public sectors. The Institute of Public Affairs, once again, has been the saving grace with critical and wise commentary during the lockdown crisis, beginning with John Roskam, Gideon Rozner and Daniel Wild.

I have discovered a great deal during this crisis and for the record, please allow me this observation:

> Forget the left-wing or right-wing categories when it comes to politics. There is now, those on the public purse and those who are not. And those on the public purse have been arrogant in their attitude towards those in the private sector.

I wonder when the next lockdown will occur, will it be over a climate change emergency? I know it is a bit extreme and maybe I am taking it a bit far, but then again, when I was in Melbourne in early March, at no point did I expect we would all be in lockdown.

I apologize for not issuing the *Connor Court Quarterly* more frequently, like I promised last time, I will try harder to get out another issue before the year it out.

OUR TEN DAYS THAT SHOOK THE WORLD

Jeffrey Tucker

First published in AIER, April 8, 2020

Jack Reed, the American communist who was buried in the Kremlin, is the author of the extremely exciting book *Ten Days that Shook the World*. It's about the Bolshevik Revolution which is witnessed first hand, and he was a huge fan who turned out to be one of many of its victims. But his book is also about any time of astonishing upheaval, times like our own when history seems to turn on a dime in ways no one expected. A quasi-free society became a

fully planned one, under the control of an elite who claimed the mantle of science.

We are living through something similar. The results have been similarly disappointing. We tried to "flatten the curve" to preserve hospital capacity, but this is just a fancy way of saying "prolong the pain." It was a form of rationing access to medical services, seemingly necessary given the scoliosis of this highly regulated industrial sector. But the political class and their modelers only considered one kind of pain. Other forms of pain are already here in the form of mass unemployment, waves of bankruptcy, rising despair, social division and anger, a panicked political class, and a seething fury on the part of millions of people – who had long taken their right to work and associate as a given – who suddenly find themselves under house arrest.

Going through my personal financial statements for the last 30 days, I'm reminded of how this nightmare unfolded.

My last trip to the old New York was on March

12. I was with AIER's videographer Taleed Brown. The virus was all the talk but the city hadn't shut down yet. There were fewer cars on the road, fewer people by half walking around. The bars were full, stuffed with people even at 11:00am who had some sense that this might be their last drink. Groups of 4 and 6 were sitting around talking and trying to celebrate birthdays and pretend things were normal, as best they could.

But things weren't normal. I was there for a 4pm television interview, and I had 5 hours to wait for it. I worried that the Amtrak would stop running before we could catch it. We would be trapped. So the minutes went by for hours. Taleed and I sat there eating and drinking but even at the Irish Pub, things were different. There were paper tablecloths where there used to be exposed wood. Our waitresses stood far away and set our drinks and food down on the table next to us. She had a look of impending doom of her face, as she confronted two possible disasters: getting sick and getting shut down.

How far along had the disease progressed at

that point? The first US case of Coronavirus was reported January 20th, in Washington State. No one knows how many other cases there were already spreading through the Northeast of the US. Thousands? Millions? Many cases have no symptoms. Others feel like a minor cold. Others are taken down for a couple of days. Do you tell others and get tested every time you feel sick? No. The virus might already have been everywhere in New York when I was there.

The interview finally came and went and we rushed to the train station to get home as soon as possible. Were we carrying infection? I had no idea. There was no means to find out. Even after all this time, there still is no widespread testing outside of hospitals. If CVS did offer the test, there would be a line down the block. The fateful disaster of the CDC/FDA to botch the creation and distribution of tests is still present in our lives.

We still don't know. Amazing.

After that day in New York, our worlds began to shut down. The following day, a national emergency was declared. Then the CDC recommended against gatherings of 50 or more people. France locked down. Borders closed. Then the unthinkable scenario unfolded: stores shut, borders shut, police-enforced stay home orders, mass unemployment, family bankruptcy, psychological depression, a nation of prisoners in our homes. Spooky doesn't describe it. Not one person in the US imagined this was possible, and I'm speaking as a person who warned of coming quarantines on January 27.

Back then, I wrote the following:

> Remember that it is not government that discovers the disease, treats the disease, keeps diseased patients from wandering around, or otherwise compels sick people to decline to escape their sick beds. Institutions do this, institutions that are part of the social order and not exogenous to it.
>
> Individuals don't like to get others sick. People don't like to get sick. Given this, we have a mechanism that actually works. Society has

an ability and power of its own to bring about quarantine-like results without introducing the risk that the State's quarantine power will be used and abused for political purposes.

But the political class in the United States (unlike Sweden and South Korea) didn't trust society. Oh, to be sure, society was trusted to adapt to the most astonishing series of mandates, burdens, and shifts in modern history. The whole of the industrial structure was massively contorted, distorted, and violently attacked. And yet the grocery stores and pharmacies, plus all their suppliers, proved unbelievably adaptable, people became specialists in distancing, and millions learned about remote work and digital hangouts.

The political elites and their plans for us just assumed society was capable of this, and they were right. But if society could achieve this level of upheaval in the course of a week, how much more capable would it have been in dealing with a disease itself – and dare I suggest deal with the disease better than

jgd graphic+web

www.jgd.com.au

Publishing Solutions ...
Book design, Prestige publications,
Annual Reports, Year Books & Magazine
production. Services include; cover & page
design, maps, charts & diagrams,
photographic art direction & illustration

Web Solutions ...
WordPress, Sitefinity & Bloomtools. Mailchimp
integration. Services include; design, project
management, construction, seo & maintenance

Video Solutions ...
Editing & Motion graphics. Social Media Ads,
Webinars with support graphics.
Supplied in Microsoft or Adobe CC

Project Quotes & Estimates ...
Ian James – 0488 069 194 (Melbourne)
Email – ian@jgd.com.au

the politicians ever could. This is precisely why 800 serious medical professionals begged and pleaded to stop the lockdown before it happened.

The trouble I had from the beginning with this whole central plan to flatten the curve – we cannot know if it is happening much less why, simply because we have neither data nor a clear test of cause and effect – is that central plans have never worked. They are hugely costly in ways that models cannot predict. Meanwhile, the medical professionals have discovered features of this disease that are distinct and should have informed policy decisions. Even after the shutdown, some politicians began to doubt. "If you rethought that or had time to analyze that public health strategy," said New York Governor Andrew Cuomo. "I don't know that you would say quarantine everyone. I don't even know that that was the best public health policy."

By then it was too late.

But let's return to Jack Reed and his dreams

for a communist world, starting with Russia. I recently re-watched the film Reds. After all these years, the movie holds up as one of the most intellectually interesting and visually powerful portrayals of lost history that I've seen.

The movie stars Warren Beatty playing John Reed, while Diane Keaton plays his girlfriend and eventual wife, Louise Bryant. It includes some of the best romantic fight scenes I've ever seen, not least because they paralleled the actual off-screen lives of Beatty and Keaton. The portrayals of figures like Max Eastman, Eugene O'Neill, and Emma Goldman are very convincing.

In terms of culture and politics, the film provides a richer education than you can get from 50 books on the topic of the Progressive Era, the Great War, the Russian Revolution, and the heady brew of interwoven cultural issues like women's suffrage, birth control, abortion, free love, and the beginnings of the organized socialist movement in the United States.

I've never been sympathetic to the Bolsheviks as

versus the old regime in Russia, but the scenes here from the revolution are completely inspired and touch the heart of anyone who agrees with Jefferson on the positive need for revolution from time to time. The portrayals of both Lenin and Trotsky seem authentic, and thrillingly so.

That sense you get that you are watching the real thing is enhanced by the extended interviews with people who actually knew both Reed and Bryant. They all have strong opinions. They are wise. They are insightful. We hear from communists and anticommunists, socialites and politicians, working-class philosophers and credentialed academics. It is a beautiful mix.

From a political perspective, the film offers a devastating turnaround judgment on the results of revolution. Emma Goldman tries to talk some sense into Reed in the years following, and explains that millions have died from starvation, that nothing works right, that the vanguard of the proletariat has become a centralized police state. Reed won't listen. He explains back to her that the socialist revolution requires terror, murder, and firing squads.

Here is the exchange with Maureen Stapleton playing Emma Goldman:

> Goldman: "Jack, we have to face it. The dream that we had is dying. If Bolshevism means the peasants taking the land, the workers taking the factories, then Russia's one place where there is no Bolshevism."
>
> Reed: "Ya know, I can argue with cops. I can fight with generals. I can't deal with a bureaucrat."
>
> Goldman: "You think Zinoviev is nothing worse than a bureaucrat. The Soviets have no local autonomy. The central state has all the power. All the power is in the hands of a few men and they are destroying the revolution. They are destroying any hope of real communism in Russia. They are putting people like me in jail. My understanding of revolution is not a continual extermination of political dissenters. And I want no part of it. Every single newspaper has been shut down or taken over by the Party. Anyone even vaguely suspected of being a counter-

John "Jack" Silas Reed (October 22, 1887 – October 17, 1920) was an American journalist, poet, and communist activist. Reed first gained prominence as a war correspondent during the first World War, and later became best known for his coverage of the October Revolution in Petrograd, Russia, which he wrote about in his book *Ten Days That Shook the World*. (Wikipedia)

revolutionary can be taken out and shot without a trial. Where does it end? Is any nightmare justifiable in the name of defense against counter-revolution? The dream may be dying in Russia, but I'm not. It may take some time, but I'm getting out."

Reed: "You sound like you are a little confused about the revolution in action, EG. Up 'till now you've only dealt with it in theory. What did you think this thing was going to be? A revolution by consensus where we all sat down and agreed over a cup of coffee?"

Goldman: "Nothing works! Four million people died last year. Not from fighting war, they died from starvation and typhus in a militaristic police state that suppresses freedom and human rights — where nothing works!"

Reed: "They died because of the French, British and American blockade that cut off all food and medical supplies. And, counter-revolutionaries have sabotaged the factories and the railroads and telephones. And the people, the poor, ignorant, superstitious, illiterate people are trying to run things themselves just like you always said they should, but they don't know how to run them yet. Did you honestly think things were going to work right away? Did you honestly expect social transformation was going to be anything other than a murderous process? It's a war EG, and we got to fight it like we fight a war: with discipline, with terror, with firing squads. Or we just give it up."

Goldman: "Those four million didn't die fighting a war. They died from a system that

> cannot work."

> Reed: "It's just the beginning EG. It's not happening like we thought it would. It's not happening the way we wanted it to, but it is happening. If you walk out on it now, what does your whole life mean?"

And here we come to understand something of the strange mind of the dedicated communist ideologue, so dogmatic in his adherence to a creed that nothing can shake his faith, not even the deaths of millions and millions of people. His doubts about the revolution and the Communist Party crystallize only when one of his speeches is edited. So he can turn a blind eye to holocaust, but a violation of his freedom to speak becomes an intolerable act. Some moral compass!

The entire story makes an interesting parallel with our own times. The barren predictive models on how many would die from the coronavirus felt like science but their range of predictions made them useless in practice. It would be like a weather prediction that said:

either your house will completely flood or there will be a light drizzle, depending on whether you do the following Kabuki dance. Still, the media howled and the politicians acted in extreme ways to protect their standing with voters (or so they believed then).

What they hadn't considered were a number of possibilities: the models weren't predictive, curve flattening is pain prolonging, the coronavirus doesn't spontaneously appear just because people are in groups, nothing about staying home is going to cause the virus to get bored and go away, the costs of unemployment and bankruptcy are astonishingly high, school closings put older vulnerable people in direct contact with children who do not suffer the effects of infection, and the whole reaction was based on a presumption that human rights and the Constitution do not matter. It was brutal, irrational, medieval, and eschewed the advice of the best and most learned minds in epidemiology.

They created madness and destruction and called it health.

THE FRIEDMAN PAPERS

Jeffrey Tucker

Paperback, 84 pages, $19.95

This exclusive ALS Friedman Conference volume is a collection of Jeffrey Tucker's writings that have been selected in order to showcase his views on a wide range of issues. In reading these pieces you will be treated to Tucker's unique insights and libertarian outlook that will leave you with a fresh new perspective. Tucker isn't afraid to talk about any topic and this volume includes pieces on cryptocurrency, sexual harassment, cultural appropriation, net neutrality, the welfare state and more. Tucker's style is friendly and conversational, and he writes always with libertarian principles firmly in the spotlight. Enjoy this first of many Friedman papers, published each year in time for the next ALS Friedman Conference.

www.connorcourtpublishing.com.au

At the end of this, there will still be Goldmans and Reeds, people who admit errors and those who will stick by their guns, humble minds who will see that there were better ways and arrogant fools who will keep screaming that setting the world on fire was all we could do.

The Goldmans will say: millions suffered not from the virus but from the response to the virus. Meanwhile, we threw out every principle of human decency, freedom, property, and science.

The Reeds will say: It didn't happen like we thought it would, but it happened. If you reject it now, what does your whole life mean?

NICOLA ROXON, HOW SMART YOU WERE

Marc Hendrickx

*First appeared in Quadrant Online,
21st April 2020*

If you want to see what a proportionate response to a pandemic looks like re-visit 2009. That was when the Swine Flu pandemic's projections posited up to 20,000 deaths in Australia, yet there were no lockdowns. AFL and the rugby codes proceeded unimpeded and no one accused solitary golfers of killing their fellow citizens, as Victoria's Daniel Andrews told the ABC just days ago. Travel and the economy were

A GUIDE TO CLIMBING AYERS ROCK

Marc Hendrickx

Foreword by Ian Plimer

Paperback with illustrations and maps, $34.95

Since the handover of Uluru – Kata Tjuta National Park to its traditional Anangu owners in 1985 "the Climb", that great Australian outback institution, undertaken by about 7 million Australian and international tourists has been neglected, disparaged, maligned and ignored by the Board and Managers of the National Park.

www.connorcourtpublishing.com.au

similarly unaffected. The exaggerated response to COVID-19 is what you get when policy is placed in the hands of bureaucrats given their head by elected leaders taking their cues from hysterics.

In coming months our politicians and bureaucrats will be busy crafting the history of *their* response to the COVID-19 pandemic. Considerable emphasis will no doubt be placed on comparing early epidemiological models, based on data from other countries, which suggested tens of thousands were at extreme risk from the virus. Indeed, exactly that spinning is now underway, with Victoria's chief medical officer, Brett Sutton, claiming on Monday that the measures he has recommended, and which the police have enforced with random stops and $1600 fines, saved 36,000 lives. Why be so modest, Dr Sutton, why not come up with some fresh modelling and claim credit for 100,000 saved lives?

It is perhaps worth noting here that, until he switched to COVID-19 alarmism, Dr Sutton was a committed propagator of the so-called "climate emergency", being the lead author of a paper published as late as March 16, which detailed how the Garden State would respond to the "existential threat" of rising temperatures. In another recent paper, Dr Sutton was at pains to stress how

by working together, we can better address the complex challenges that climate change presents, safeguard our prosperity, and ensure Victoria continues to be one of the most sustainable and liveable places in the world.

Read that excerpt with an eye for irony in light of the current anti-COVID measures and you'll find it hard not to wear a grim smile, not least at the enthusiasm with which Dr Sutton flings himself and his models at every latest "existential threat". As for "safeguarding our prosperity", he really should have a chat with some of the newly unemployed. They could have a coffee together — no, wait, the cafes are all shut, and if they repaired to a local park VicPol would swoop with fine books at the ready.

Yes, history will be written by officials keen to justify their policies and the economic disaster that has ensued, the extreme lockdowns and abuse of civil liberties to enforce them. What we can count on is of them making no mention by way of comparison with that Swine Flu of 2009? The Rudd Government was in office at the time and its response — credit where credit is due — should have provided some lessons applicable to our current circumstances.

Swine Flu infected between 700 million and 1400 million people globally (the estimates vary), the higher number representing as much as 21 per cent of the global population. The fatality estimates are similarly broad, with somewhere between 150,000 and 575,000 thought to have been killed. Epidemiological models of the Swine Flu pandemic suggested Australian deaths would be in the order of 20,000. The Rudd Government, surprisingly, ignored the worst of the models while still planning for up to 6000 deaths. There are other differences between then and now. Unlike COVID-19, which harvests the bulk of its lives from the ranks of the elderly, Swine Flu afflicted the young, the median age of those Australians whose lives it claimed being 48. Infants and young children were among those killed.

By the end of 2009, around 38,000 Australians had been infected and there were 191 dead, a crude death rate of 0.9 per 100,000. The disease had a hospitalisation rate of 13 per cent, with 13 per cent of those admitted needing to be placed in intensive care. Despite the rate of infections and deaths, the Rudd Government did not impose any restrictions on movement or force businesses to close. Restaurants, bars and clubs remained open and profitable. Beaches and parks were not closed. The public was able to barrack at the footy, play sport, go fishing, and wash their cars without the risk of being fined by revenuers in blue. There were no restrictions on interstate or overseas travel. Even with the aftershocks of the Global Financial Crisis unfolding, Australia's unemployment rate in 2009 remained below 6 per cent. There was no economic or social meltdown. There were no outcries from the media or public for the government to do more, to adopt any measure that might save an additional life, not even with small children and mums-to-be succumbing.

By comparison COVID-19 has thus far officially infected less than 7000 and killed 72 (April 21), according to the latest data. As of April 16, the median age of the dead was 79. Remarkably, no Australia under 50 has thus far died from the disease. The crude death rate of COVID-19 in Australia stands at just 0.25 per 100,000. In 2009, despite experts predicting up to 20,000 deaths, Kevin Rudd offered little more than basic hygiene advice – wash your hands. By contrast, the economic impact of the measures implemented by state and federal governments to save Australians from COVID-19 is measured in the hundreds of billions of dollars. We could see as much as a 22 per cent drop in GDP. After a month of lockdowns the unemployment rate is already over 10 per cent and is expected to rise to figures last seen during the Great Depression. The contrast in responses and consequences given the similar magnitude of today's threat and that of 2009 could not be more stark.

The current government's modelling that showed a health system overwhelmed with

Covid-19 cases if nothing were done was based on deeply flawed inputs that assumed the virus' local impact would mirror the disastrous tolls in Italy and Spain. Various *Quadrant* contributors, Peter Smith most notably, have pointed out that rates of transmission and death in jurisdictions with dense and highly concentrated populations, especially those with large cadres of the elderly, is to compare apples with oranges.

The so-far mild impact of COVID-19 in Australia could have been predicted, or at least anticipated as a likely possibility, based on Australia's unique geography, demographics, lifestyle and season. The virus arrived at the end of summer, the weather still warm and with the flu season, which typically kills around 3000 Australians per year, still months away. Our generally healthy population resides for the most part in sprawling suburbs of stand-alone homes. Yes, Australians *do* live in apartments, but even where the density is high it remains slight by comparison with, say, New York, where COVID-19 is taking a much higher toll.

We have low rates of smoking. Our frail and elderly largely live isolated from the rest of us in nursing homes, and the next most vulnerable group of independent retirees reside in their own homes, mostly away from family, unlike Italy and Spain. If these factors were taken into account by the modellers, insufficient weight was accorded them.

Models are only as good as the data they are fed — and the number-crunching bureaucrats fed their epidemiological models on junk food. Unfortunately no single politician exercised any critical thinking and the flawed models, adopted as gospel truth, were b roadcast to a worried public. "Flatten the curve" became the law of the land, with no serious questions being raised. In 2009, Rudd's health minister, Nicola Roxon, ignored expert epidemiological models that predicted 20,000 Swine Flu deaths. Many *Quadrant* readers will likely think poorly of Rudd & Co., but credit where it is due: when the panic merchants came calling, Ms Roxon sent them on their way with the sheaves of dire predictions they rode in on.

The current pandemic could have been successfully handled with increased public awareness of hygiene, appropriate distancing and protection of the most vulnerable without resorting to the extreme measures that have created the dystopian world in which we are now forced to reside. The number of deaths would likely be a little higher, but not much more than those of 2009.

The response to Swine Flu vs COVID-19 is mystifying. How can the government say its response has been proportionate to the level of risk when the risk-reward assessment was never done? How, in just ten short years, did we discard the pragmatic and rational response to one virus with a declared man-the-battle-stations "health emergency"? How is that a minister in an incompetent Labor government could see through flawed advice, yet a Coalition government which bills itself as better and sharper managers swallowed hook, line and sinker?

Later, as the "experts" re-write history to the advantage of their conduct when COVID-19 came to town, these are questions it behooves Australians now being fined and confined to keep very much at front of mind.

AN EGREGIOUS STATISTICAL HORROR STORY SUFFUSED WITH INCENSE AND LUGUBRIOUS ACCENTS

Jeffrey Tucker

Reprinted from <u>RealClearMarkets</u>

With the latest reports of plummeting death rates from all causes, this crisis is over. The pandemic of doom erupted as a panic of pols and is now a comedy of Mash-minded med admins and stooges, covering their ifs ands and butts with ever more morbid and distorted statistics.

The crisis now will hit the politicians and political Doctor Faucis who gullibly accepted and trumpeted what statistician William Briggs calls "the most colossal and costly blown forecast of all time."

An egregious statistical horror story of millions of projected deaths, suffused with incense and lugubrious accents from Imperial College of London to Harvard School of Public Health, prompted the pols to impose a vandalistic lockdown on the economy. It would have been an outrage even if the assumptions were not wildly astronomically wrong.

Flattening the curve was always a fool's errand that widened the damage.

President Trump had better take notice. He will soon own this gigantic botch of policy and leadership. No one will notice that his opponents urged even more panicky blunders.

The latest figures on overall death rates from all causes show no increase at all. Deaths are lower than in 2019, 2018, 2017 and 2015, slightly higher than in 2016. Any upward bias is imparted by population growth.

Now writing a book on the crisis with bestselling author Jay Richards, Briggs concludes: "Since pneumonia deaths are up, yet all deaths are down, it must mean people are being recorded as dying from other things at smaller rates than usual." Deaths from other causes are simply being ascribed to the coronavirus.

As usual every year, deaths began trending downward in January. It's an annual pattern. Look it up. Since the lockdown began in mid-March, the politicians cannot claim that their policies had anything to do with the declining death rate.

A global study published in Israel by Professor Isaac Ben-Israel, chairman of the Israeli Space Agency and Council on Research and Development, shows that "the spread of the coronavirus declines to almost zero after 70 days—no matter where it strikes, and no matter what measures governments impose to try to thwart it."

In fact, by impeding herd immunity, particularly among students and other non-susceptible young people, the lockdown in the U.S. has prolonged and exacerbated the medical problem. As Briggs concludes, "People need to get out into virus-killing sunshine and germicidal air."

This flu like all previous viral flues will give way only to herd immunity, whether through natural propagation of an extremely infectious pathogen, or through the success of one of the hundreds of vaccine projects.

No evidence indicates that this flu was exceptionally dangerous. On March 20th, the French published a major controlled study that shows no excess mortality at all from coronavirus compared to other flues. SARS and Mers were both much more lethal and did not occasion what Briggs' reader "Uncle Dave" described as "taking a hammer and sickle to the economy."

We now know that the crisis was a comedy of errors. The Chinese let it get going in the raw bat markets of Wuhan. But together with the Koreans, the Chinese dithered and demurred and allowed six weeks of rampant propagation to create herd immunity before they began locking everyone up. Therefore, the Chinese and Koreans were among the first to recover.

The Italians scared everybody with their haphazard health system and smoking fogies. Crammed together in subways and tenements, the New Yorkers registered a brief blip of extreme cases. Intubations and ventilators turned out not to help (80 percent died). This sowed fear and frustration among medical personnel slow to see that the problem was impaired hemogloblin in the blood rather than lung damage.

The New York media piled on with panic, with bogus reports of rising deaths. "Coronavirus deaths" soared by assuming that people dying with the virus were dying from it and then by ascribing to the coronavirus other deaths among people with symptoms of pulmonary distress, even without being tested.

Now jacking up the case rate will be further

pointless testing. As Briggs points out, "Fauci is calling for 'tripling' of testing, which can only boost these dailies [case totals]. And make it seem like there's a genuine increase occurring. Oh my! The daily reported cases are up! It must mean the disease is spreading!

"No. It could also mean, and probably does given all the other evidence we now have from sampling, that the disease was already there, and we just now have measured it."

The death rate rises with further reclassification of pneumonia and other pulmonary deaths. When we reach herd immunity, and nearly everyone has the antigen, nearly all deaths can be chalked up to COVID19. Hey, it will be Quod Erat Demonstrandum for the panic mongers.

In a fascinating open letter to German Prime Minister Angela Merkel, epidemiologist Mihai Grigorius concludes that with the French study, corroborated by findings from a Stanford antibody seroprevalence study in Santa Clara county, "the case for extreme measures collapses like a house of cards." Grigorius says that since the virus has already spread widely in the general population, efforts to stop further spread are both futile and destructive.

So let's stop pretending that our policies have been rational and need to be phased out, as if they once had a purpose. They should be reversed summarily and acknowledged to be a mistake, perpetrated by statisticians with erroneous computer models.

Perhaps then we can learn from this experience with the flaws of expertise not to shut down the economy again for the totally bogus "crisis" of climate change.

WHY AUSTRALIA NEEDS EQUALITY OF SACRIFICE

Daniel Wild

29 April 2020

FROM THE IPA TODAY,
PUBLICATIONS, RESEARCH AREAS

You will read about how, for the first time in Australia, IPA research has demonstrated the rapid growth and complexity of environmental regulation, and how this is stopping $65 billion worth of job-creating investment in Australia's regions.

How the Next Generation Faces more Debt and Higher Taxes

Long after the health impacts of COVID-19 have passed, the legacy of the necessary but costly government economic rescue and stimulus packages will remain with us through the accumulation of record levels of public debt.

Research Fellow Cian Hussey was the first to undertake economic modelling which forecast that gross Commonwealth government debt would reach $1 trillion within three years. As Cian's analysis of 1 April found, total gross Commonwealth debt prior to the crisis was already $556 billion. To that, some $230 billion in fiscal spending measures had been announced by the Commonwealth government, meaning debt would increase by 41 per cent to $786 billion.

Cian also estimated that there would be at least $250 billion in lost revenue and higher expenses over the next three years due to the depressed economic activity resulting from social isolation measures, bringing total debt to over $1 trillion.

Cian estimated that paying off the debt will cost $30,600 for each Australian.

To put this into further context, John Roskam estimated in analysis for the Australian Financial Review that even if the interest payments on this debt is "only" one per cent, that still equates to $400 each year for each Australian. And as interest rates inevitably normalise, those interest payments will continue to grow.

The rapid accumulation of debt also demonstrates the abdication of economic leadership since the GFC. That more than half of the forecast accumulation to debt occurred prior to the present crisis, and during 28 years of unbroken headline economic growth, shows that Australia's political class has badly mismanaged the public finances of Australia. Many Australians would be willing to tolerate the debt accumulated during this crisis as the cost of an unforeseen public health crisis that necessitated extraordinary government intervention.

But the failure to get the debt burden under

control during good economic times is unforgivable.

IPA research and analysis sparked a broader public debate about how Australia can pay off this debt – and that is by growing the economy by becoming more productive.

Over recent weeks the debate has broadened into commentary about "economic reform". I must admit that I have never liked the word reform because it is ambiguous. Reform could mean higher taxes and more regulation, or shutting down coal-fired power stations, for example. The carbon tax and the NBN were billed as "reform" measures.

The Australian economy doesn't need reform, it needs lower taxes, less red and green tape, lower electricity prices, a small and less interventionist bureaucracy, and a flexible and decentralised industrial relations system.

Public debt doesn't just matter for economic or financial reasons. It also matters for moral reasons. The trillion dollars in Commonwealth public debt will ultimately be paid back by today's young Australians through higher taxes, making it harder for them to get a job or start a business.

Promoting Jobs in the Private Economy

Jobs will be the most important factor in the recovery of the Australian economy and society from state and federal government-imposed social isolation measures put in place to manage the spread of COVID-19. The more Australians who stay in their job throughout the lockdown period, the quicker and stronger the recovery will be.

IPA research and analysis has identified that environmental regulation and red tape, often referred to as "green tape", is a major impediment to business investment and job creation in Australia. Two pieces of IPA research have highlighted this as a part of the IPA's Cut Red Tape for Australia's Jobs research program.

Environmental "Lawfare" is Stopping

Investment and Jobs

Environmental activists such as the Australian Conservation Foundation have used a special legal privilege called Section 487 to put at risk $65 billion of investment by holding major projects in court for a cumulative total of 10,100 days since the year 2000. That is the key finding of the latest research report by Research Fellow Kurt Wallace, Section 487: How Activists use Red Tape to Stop Development and Jobs (2020 update).

Some prominent examples of affected projects include a $30 billion mine expansion of the Olympic Dam mine by BHP, Adani's $16.5 billion coal mine, a $2.3 billion Tasmanian pulp mill, the $767 million Maules Creek mine, and the $240 million Anvil Hill coal mine.

Under Section 487 of the Environment Protection and Biodiversity Conservation Act 1999 (EPBC Act) environmental activist groups are able to challenge the ministerial approval of projects which could have a major impact on a matter of national environmental significance. There are nine such matters, including nationally threatened species and ecological communities, migratory species, and a water resource in relation to coal seam gas development and large coal mining development.

The notional objective of Section 487 is to provide a legal avenue for environmental groups to ensure that ministerial approvals of major projects are being made consistent with the provisions set out in the EPBC Act. But Kurt's research found that what is actually happening is Section 487 is being used to launch frivolous and vexatious lawsuits – often referred to as "lawfare" – which are very rarely successful in court.

Kurt analysed the annual reports of the federal environment department over the past two decades, as well as all the judgments handed down under Section 487 and found that since 2000:

- 41 cases have proceeded to judgment.
- A further 10 legal challenges were discontinued or withdrawn.

- Seven cases resulted in changes to the original ministerial approval.

- Only three of the changed approvals resulted in a substantial change in conditions.

- This means that 94 per cent of cases have not led to substantial environmental changes.

The very low success rate does not mean that there is a correspondingly small impact on the projects which are subject to legal challenge. Far from it. Environmental groups can take advantage of the asymmetric nature of the costs imposed by legal action. The critical factor for environmental groups is not to win the court cases, but to engage in as much litigation as possible and to draw this out for as long as possible to disrupt and delay economic development. The proponents of legal action do not need to win the court case to succeed in their broader ideological objectives. It is the process which is the punishment.

At worst, the environmental groups undertaking legal action must pay the costs of court action. But the direct costs of court action are dwarfed by the economic and social costs of forgone business investment and job creation.

This asymmetric nature of the costs of court action is precisely what environmental groups have knowingly and methodically exploited to pursue their ideological goals. Greenpeace Australia, for example, authored the strategy document Stopping the Australian Coal Export Boom which states that "our vision for the Australian anti-coal movement is that it that functions like an orchestra, with a large number of different voices combining together into a beautiful symphony (or a deafening cacophony!)."

The key strategy outlined is to 'disrupt and delay' key projects, while gradually eroding public and political support for the coal industry. To do this, green groups will "get in front of the critical projects to slow them down in the approval process" by undertaking "significant investment in legal capacity" in order to engage in sustained legal battles.

Green Tape Continues to Grow – But There is Hope

IPA Research Fellow Cian Hussey found in his latest report, The Growth and Complexity of Environmental Law, that federal environmental regulation contained in the EPBC Act has grown by 445 per cent since the year 2000. That is an average annual growth rate of 10.4 per cent, compared with an average annual economic growth rate of 2.9 per cent and population growth rate of 1.5 per cent over the same period.

What is so important about Cian's research is that it digs beneath the surface and not only analyses the headline federal environmental regulations, but all the departmental and subsidiary regulations which they enable. As Cian explains, the primary mechanism for introducing new rules is through legislation passed by parliament. This is what is debated and what the public is often informed about. But this legislation also enables ministers to create or change rules through "subsidiary legislation" which is not subject to the same parliamentary oversight and, in the case of federal environmental law, is responsible for more regulation than the initial legislation passed by parliament. This is a huge democratic accountability problem and leads to a type of rule by bureaucrats and "experts".

As the title of the report suggests, Cian also analysed the complexity of environmental law – and for the first time was able to quantitatively demonstrate the complexity of federal environmental regulations. Often those subject to environmental regulation, such as farmers, make the observation that it is difficult and sometimes impossible for them to comply with their regulatory obligations because of the sheer volume and complexity of those obligations. Cian found that these observations are well-founded.

Cian employed four quantitative methods to analyse complexity: the Shannon Entropy method which measures how likely readers of a text are to encounter new words and concepts; the Flesh Reading Ease method which measures how easy a document is to read and understand; the number of "conditionals" used in sentences such as "ifs", "buts", and "excepts" – more conditions makes a document harder to read; and average sentence length.

Three key research findings are:

> A Shannon Entropy score of 9.48, which means that readers of the EPBC Act are more likely to encounter new words and concepts than readers of Shakespeare's plays such as Romeo and Juliet.
>
> The EPBC Act contains 2,057 conditionals compared to the average piece of federal legislation of 88.
>
> The EPBC Act has an average sentence length of 48.41 words, compared with the average piece of federal legislation average of 34.67. By comparison, A Tale of Two Cities by Charles Dickens, the popular Victorian-era author who was paid per word, has an average sentence length of 17.7 words.

I mentioned in my last email about how the IPA is working with leading economists at the US-based Mercatus Center at George Mason University on our economics and regulation research programs. Cian's report employs what is called the 'RegData' methodology that was developed by the Mercatus Center and brought to Australia by the IPA and our colleagues at RMIT University.

RegData uses machine learning and textual analysis to count the number of 'regulatory restrictions' contained in a given piece of legislation or subsidiary legislation. Regulatory restrictions are clauses in legislation and subsidiary legislation which compel or prevent certain behaviours. There are five such clauses captured by the RegData methodology: "shall", "must", "may not", "prohibited", and "required".

I mentioned in the title of this section that while environmental regulation has grown, there is hope. The reason I say this is because Cian's report, which was released only last week, has already had a big impact. In response to the release of Cian's report which was covered in The Australian on 24 April, the federal environment minister Sussan Ley stated that the government is "set to cut green tape in time for October's post-coronavirus federal budget."

Cian makes a number of very important recommendations of where the government might like to start:

The total volume of regulation contained within the EPBC Act and associated subsidiary legislation should be returned to the year 2000 levels. This would mean a reduction in the number of regulatory restrictions from 4,820 to 855, an 82 per cent reduction.

Section 487 of the EPBC Act should be repealed.

The 'water trigger' should be removed from the list of Matters of National Environmental Significance which would allow more coal and coal seam gas projects to be undertaken.

Section 140A of the EPBC Act, which prohibits the development of nuclear power in Australia, should be repealed.

The EPBC Act should focus on localism and decentralisation to remove duplication and leave environmental regulation with states, territories, and the communities directly affected by such regulation.

Regulation under the EPBC Act should focus on environmental outcomes, rather than compliance with a process.

Cian's report was submitted to the decadal review of the EPBC Act. Submissions closed two weeks ago, and the panel is now preparing its final report and will undertake a series of hearings. I will keep you updated on the IPA's engagement.

Defending Freedom and Democracy

Australia is a fortunate and proud custodian of the ancient rights and liberties that were won and negotiated by the British people dating back hundreds of years at least to Magna Carta in 1215. That charter provided for limited forms of religious liberty, political representation for those paying tax, and protection from illegal imprisonment. Those limited rights and liberties have today grown to the far broader freedoms of speech, association, religion, the rule of law, legal rights such as the presumption of innocence, and representative parliamentary democracy.

It is true that the potential health crisis posed by the spread of the coronavirus necessitated abnormal government intervention through social isolation measures. But a health crisis, or any crisis, should never be used as a pretext for putting democracy and freedom on hiatus, which is precisely what has happened in Australia over the past month and in particular in Victoria and New South Wales.

Research Fellow Morgan Begg analysed the different social isolation restrictions imposed by state governments in his report States of Emergency: An Analysis of Covid-19 Petty Restrictions. To do this Morgan analysed the directions issued by state premiers and state chief medical officers under emergency declarations. Morgan's report contains several important findings.

The first is the dramatic inconsistency in

restrictions across different state governments. It is true that Australia is a federation, and so state governments should have wide discretion in terms of public policy, including in relation to emergency health issues. But it is unclear why, as Morgan found, fishing by yourself is banned in Victoria but allowed in NSW provided appropriate social distancing is practiced; or why social visits of immediate family members who do not live together are not allowed in Victoria unless for compassionate reasons, but a gathering of up to 10 people is allowed in South Australia; or why it is illegal to sit idly on a park bench in NSW or Victoria but no specific direction is provided in WA, SA, or Tasmania.

The second key finding of Morgan's report is that many of the social isolation rules undermine Australians' legal rights. Morgan argues that:

> "The implementation of these rules is often arbitrary and inconsistent with the fundamental legal rights of Australians, such as the presumption of innocence. A violation of a direction issued under public health or emergency powers will result in a strict

> liability offence. This means that the state does not need to find a mental element, or a person's intention to commit a crime, in order to be issued a penalty."

This means that in practice people who are outside of the house would in many instances be required to justify why they are outside or being with or around other people.

Morgan's report and associated analysis Morgan provided for The Spectator Australia raises deeper questions about the role of experts and parliamentary accountability. Even if one were to accept the premise of social distancing, it is not immediately apparent how undertaking activities by oneself or with appropriate social distancing measures could contribute to the spread of coronavirus. As Morgan argues, "many of the strict rules imposed by state governments have failed to take into consideration whether those activities can be undertaken while maintaining distancing of 1.5 metres." In other words, there appears to be a bias towards banning economic and social activity, rather than permitting activity that can fit within the framework of 1.5 metre distancing and sensible personal hygiene.

A part of the explanation is that Australia's normal parliamentary processes have been suspended or severely truncated. The vast majority of the social distancing measures have been passed by declaration rather than through laws passed by parliament. For example, federal parliament was suspended on 23 March and will not return until the 12th of May when for three days, according to reporting in The Australian, a number of "COVID-19 bills" will be presented to the House or Representatives. It is unclear at this stage when parliament will resume its normal business.

Some have suggested that in this extraordinary time the usual workings of Australia's parliamentary democracy should be put on hold so that urgent measures can be introduced without the usual debate and scrutiny. I could not disagree more. Scrutiny and debate are important feature of our liberal democracy, and is more important than ever when the stakes are so high and so many Australians lives are being impacted in a deep and profound way.

If parliaments across Australia sat throughout World War II, then they should be sitting now.

Equality of Sacrifice is Needed to Protect the Australian Way of Life

One of the fundamental dividing lines throughout the coronavirus lockdown period are those who have a job and those who do not and, more broadly, those who are exposed to the economic and social fallout and those who are sheltered from it.

While many of the social isolation measures have been necessary and effective, they have also been the subject of excess and overreach, as documented in the aforementioned report by Morgan. One of the reasons for this is that those who are imposing and proposing these measures are often not those who suffer the negative consequences. Public servants, bureaucrats, medical experts, academics, politicians and their staffers are largely protected from job losses and wage cuts. Whereas small business owners, front line administrative staff, families with a mortgage, tradespeople, and low-to-medium skilled white-collar professions have suffered first and suffered most – many of those who, essentially, work within or who are exposed to the private and productive economy.

In analysis I prepared for The Australian I argued that "the economic and social burden of the government-imposed sanctions to manage the health crisis must be shared equally with the public sector, which so far has remained shielded from the fallout."

I proposed seven modest measures to cut inefficient and wasteful government spending worth $30bn which could be redirected to help fund the commonwealth government's economic recovery packages.

The main part of my analysis focussed on the wage differential between public and private sector workers. Public servants on average have higher wages and higher superannuation contributions than private sector workers in Australia. I have never understood why this is the case because public sector workers are also in a less risky occupation in terms both of health and safety matters and job security.

According to the Australian Bureau of Statistics, average weekly private sector earnings are 20 per cent lower than in the public sector, implying a $4.4bn annual commonwealth public service wage premium (20 per cent of the total Commonwealth public sector wage bill of $22.12bn).

Commonwealth public servants also receive at least 15.4 per cent superannuation, compared with 9.5 per cent for private sector workers, implying a $1.3bn annual Commonwealth public service superannuation premium. Further, the 15.4 per cent superannuation contribution is paid for by taxpayers and is not funded via lower take-home public sector pay, whereas the 9.5 per cent private sector superannuation contribution is paid via lower private sector wages.

The combined public sector wage premium therefore sits at $5.7bn each year, which (at an annual salary of $80,000) would be equivalent to 71,250 jobs in the private sector.

I also analysed the 2018 annual Australia Public Service Commissioner's Remuneration Report and found an egregious example of public sector overpayment. One middle manager (referred to as an Executive Level Two) received an annual salary of $934,612 in 2018. This included a "retention bonus" of $91,196, which is higher than Australia's median salary.

As I argued "no one in the public service should be receiving a productivity or retention bonus until the crisis is over and the unemployment rate drops below 5 per cent."

The point is not to needlessly punish public servants, but to recognise that Australia is currently going through one of its greatest peace-time challenges since Federation, and that all Australians must be in this fight together. More importantly, I am concerned about what may happen to the public's confidence in our democratic institutions when they see that hard-working and risk-taking entrepreneurs are losing their jobs and having their pay cut while risk-averse public servants are as wealthy and as powerful as ever before.

I will end this email with an article that I think everyone should read which goes directly to the issue of shared sacrifice. One of the important tasks that IPA researchers perform is staying informed about the best analysis that is being undertaken in Australian and overseas.

One recent piece of analysis that we have been discussing around the office is this piece by Joel Kotkin, The Two Middle Classes, published in Quillette earlier this year. Kotkin, who is the executive director of the Urban Reform Institute based in Houston, Texas, argues there are now two distinct and opposing middle classes.

> "First there is the yeomanry or the traditional middle class, which consists of small business owners, minor landowners, craftspeople, and artisans, or what we would define historically as the bourgeoisie, or the old French Third

> Estate, deeply embedded in the private economy. The other middle class, now in ascendency, is the clerisy, a group that makes its living largely in quasi-public institutions, notably universities, media, the non-profit world, and the upper bureaucracy."

It is that first middle class that is experiencing the negative social and economic effects of the coronavirus lockdown measures, and the second middle class that is largely sheltered from, if not actively befitting from, the measures.

Shared sacrifice between those two middle classes is not only an economic issue, but a democratic imperative.

EDITORIAL BYTE

"There are obviously considerations that need to be given around privacy, and all these considerations around proportionality are actually requirements in the legislation" -- Jenny Mikakos, pictured above.

The Victorian Health Minister on why she didn't name the Meat Works factory at the centre of a fresh COVID-19 outbreak.

This same company happens to be a financial supporter of the Australian Labor Party. One is not suggesting there is a connection.

Victorian Opposition leader on Sky News: "Mr O'Brien said the Victorian government had been 'very quick to pull the trigger to name primary schools, aged care facilities, and hospitals' as it should have done, but was 'so keen to keep secret the name' of this outbreak."

ABOUT THE CONTRIBUTORS

Jeffrey Tucker

Editorial Director, American Institute for Economic Research https://www.aier.org/staff/jeffrey-tucker

Jeffrey Tucker is a former Director of Content for the Foundation for Economic Education. He is the Editorial Director at the American Institute for Economic Research, a managing partner of Vellum Capital, the founder of Liberty.me.

Marc Hendrickx

Geologist and frequent contributor to *Quadrant Online* and author of *A Guide to Climbing Ayers Rock*.

Daniel Wild

Daniel Wild is the Director of Research at the Institute of Public Affairs. He specialises in red tape, regulation, economic policy, the philosophy of free enterprise, and criminal justice. Daniel has authored research papers on economic policy, environmental regulation, and criminal justice reform.

www.ingramcontent.com/pod-product-compliance
Lightning Source LLC
Chambersburg PA
CBHW021559110426
42742CB00042B/3408